Anonymus

The Ven. John Baptist de la Salle

The true friend of youth

Anonymus

The Ven. John Baptist de la Salle
The true friend of youth

ISBN/EAN: 9783741178542

Manufactured in Europe, USA, Canada, Australia, Japa

Cover: Foto ©Thomas Meinert / pixelio.de

Manufactured and distributed by brebook publishing software
(www.brebook.com)

Anonymus

The Ven. John Baptist de la Salle

– THE –

VEN. JOHN BAPTIST DE LA SALLE,

THE TRUE FRIEND OF YOUTH,

FOUNDER OF THE

BROTHERS OF THE CHRISTIAN SCHOOLS.

NEW YORK:

DE LA SALLE INSTITUTE,

44—50 SECOND STREET.

1885.

—INSTITUTE—

BROTHERS OF THE CHRISTIAN SCHOOLS.

----◆-◆◆-◆----

Prospectus of the Novitiate.

The Institute of the Brothers of the Christian Schools, which has its Mother House at 27 Rue Oudinot, Paris, is a religious congregation, the object of which is the sanctification of its members and the Christian education of youth, especially the poor.

This Institute was founded in 1680 by the Venerable John Baptist de la Salle, and it was approved as a religious congregation by our Holy Father Benedict XIII. in the Bull, IN APOSTOLICÆ DIGNITATIS SOLIO, given on the 7th day of the calends of February, in the year of the Incarnation, 1724, (January 25th, 1725.)

The establishments conducted by the Brothers of the Christian Schools comprise gratuitous schools, orphanages, reformatories, art and agricultural schools ; also academies, colleges and normal schools for lay-teachers.

From sixteen to twenty-five is the most appropriate age for the admission of candidates. Educated men can be admitted at a more advanced age.

Boys of about fourteen are admitted in the Preparatory Novitiate, to test their vocations.

The qualities indispensably required in those who apply for admission are : 1st. Good health and fair appearance. 2d. A sound judgment, with the ability to make the required studies. 3d. Good character, control of temper, a docile and sociable disposition, detachment from worldly goods and interests, zeal for the glory of God, for the salvation of children, and one's own perfection.

The principal impediments to the admission of candidates are: Illegitimacy; bad reputation of the family; necessity of providing for parents; any grave and apparent deformity, deafness, or bad sight; inability to pay debts contracted personally; obligation to discharge the duty of guardian, or the management of property; condemnation by civil authority for some misdemeanor.

The time of probation is two years: the first in the Novitiate, the second either in the scholasticate, school, or in any other position assigned.

A candidate who is at least eighteen years of age, and who during his trial of two years has given satisfaction, may be admitted to annual vows.

Those only are admitted to triennial and perpetual vows whose application to duty and observance of Rule entitle them to that favor.

Every candidate is required, on entering the Novitiate, to bring with him the following papers: 1st. A letter of recommendation from his pastor. 2d. His Baptismal certificate. 3d. The consent, in writing, of his parents, if he is a minor.

The board for the first year is $200. This sum should be paid on entering the Novitiate. Candidates unable to pay will communicate with the Brother Visitor of the district, or his representatives.

If the candidate leave before the expiration of the first year, a proportionate sum will be charged for the time he has spent in the Novitiate.

The outfit consists of the following articles :

Six linen shirts, four undershirts, four pairs of drawers, twelve handkerchiefs, six towels, six pairs of socks, two or three complete suits of clothes, of which one is to be black, two black neckties, two pairs of shoes. These articles should be new or in good condition.

After the year of probation, the Institute bears the expense of maintaining the subject, both in sickness and in health, as also the expenses necessary for his training and studies ; but it reserves to itself the right of requiring his withdrawal for what it may judge sufficient cause.

If a Brother should leave the congregation or be expelled from it (whether he has vows or not), for any of the causes mentioned in the Rules, he has no right to, and cannot legally claim either indemnity or pension or assistance of any kind, whatever may have been his position in the Institute, or the length of time spent in it; for it is well understood that all duties are to be accepted and discharged gratuitously through a pure zeal for the glory of God and the welfare of our neighbor.

On the other hand, the congregation will not make any claim upon him for expenses occasioned by his studies, training and support.

Particulars may be obtained at any of the establishments of the Institute. Application can also be made to the Brother Visitor of the District or to the Brother Director of the Novitiate.

Novitiates of the Institute have been established in this country in Amawalk, Westchester Co., N. Y., Baltimore, St. Louis and San Francisco.

PREPARATORY NOVITIATE.

The Preparatory Novitiates are schools annexed to our Novitiates, in which boys of about fourteen years of age, who wish to embrace the religious life, are received and wherein the course of studies and religious exercises are suited to their age.

Those boys only whose conduct gives signs of vocation can be admitted to the Novitiate. Arrangements for their board are made with their parents or guardians. The other conditions are the same as those for postulants to the Novitiate.

All extra expenses are charged to parents until the candidates enter the Novitiate.

Form to be Filled by the Parents or Guardians.

I, the undersigned,*........ ....

living........................ .. . .

after having carefully read the above prospectus, consent that†

......who is my ....becomes a member of the Institute

of the Brothers of the Christian Schools..... ....

Done at........................ . ...

on the............day of.....................18....

* Name and surname of the parent or guardian.
† Name and surname of candidate.

VENERABLE JOHN BAPTIST DE LA SALLE,

The True Friend of Youth. Founder of the Brothers of the Christian Schools.

THE HOUSE IN WHICH THE VENERABLE DE LA SALLE WAS BORN.

I.

Among the illustrious names in the firmament of Catholic history none shines with greater brilliancy

than that of the Venerable John Baptist De La Salle.
The great and glorious work he was to accomplish was
foreshadowed in him from birth. From the earliest
dawn of reason he showed remarkable piety, gentleness and urbanity. Blessed with fervent, God-fearing
parents, his eager soul drank in with avidity their holy
teachings, and while yet young in years, he became mature in heavenly wisdom and understanding.

At an early age he entered the University of Rheims.
Here with his surpassing talents and unwearied application he made such rapid progress in his studies that he
distanced all his companions. This might have roused
their jealousy against him, but his gentle, winning ways
gained their affection, and none rejoiced more than
they at his success. When but sixteen years old, his
worth was so well known that the Chancellor of the University and Archdeacon of Champagne, Pierre Dozet,
who had been canon for over fifty years, chose him
as his successor in the canonry. In his humility La
Salle would have refused the honor, but through
obedience was obliged to accept it. The way he filled
the office fully justified the Chancellor's choice. In
1670, having graduated at the University of Rheims,
he went to the Seminary of St. Sulpice, in Paris, to pursue his theological studies under the best masters
of the times. In this beloved retreat, where as
everywhere else he gained the love and respect of
all, by the holiness of his life and the angelic sweetness
of his disposition, he remained till the death of his
father, following close on that of his mother, called
him home. In dying his father had left his other
children, six in number, to his care. He could not refuse so holy a legacy, though for one of his years (he
was then but twenty) it entailed heavy responsibilities.

It was now he experienced for the first time in his life a violent temptation against his vocation. There was much in his position to disturb his mind. Thus far he had received but minor orders and was not irrevocably bound to the service of the altar. How, he asked himself, could he reconcile the administration of the large fortune left by his parents with those duties which would be incumbent upon him, if he pursued his ecclesiastical career? Might he not secure his salvation in the world? Did not duty call upon him to forego his personal inclination towards a more perfect state that he might give himself up to the task of educating and protecting the young family by whom he was surrounded?

Young reader! Here is a lesson which you should carry with you through life. When nature pleads so eloquently, when the world comes in with its subtle argument, be not your own guide. Follow the example of the noble youth, De La Salle. Seek like him the protection of Mary ; cast yourself at the feet of Christ's minister, and listen to his words. To Father Roland, his confessor, John Baptiste made known the secret thoughts which strove to obtain the mastery. He pleaded not in favor of one side more than another. His motives were most pure, his sole desire was to know the Divine will which, in all future years, "he will adore in his regard." The experienced spiritual director soon learned the value of the soul he was to save from a false step : he had no hesitancy in assuring him that God required his undivided love and service. Moreover, properly directed, and with a purified intention, the distractions inevitable in his guardianship would become a source of sanctification instead of being a cause of falling away. Such was M. Roland's opinion.

This advice, which De La Salle received as an expression of the Divine will, put an end to his perplexities. While devoting himself unreservedly to the welfare of his youthful wards, he resumed his studies for the priesthood. The habits of order and discipline which were always familiar to him, but which had been strengthened by his sojourn at St.

DE LA SALLE INVOKING DIVINE AID.

Sulpice, taught him the value of a systematic mode of life at home. Accordingly, he gave his brothers and sisters a regulation in which all the hours of the day had their allotted duties or privileges.

Thus the holy youth spent six years in the quiet pursuit of his duty to his relatives and of the studies which were to prepare him for his ecclesiastical calling. In 1678 he was ordained priest. Eighteen days after his ordination M. Roland, his faithful friend, his wise and discreet director, was called to a glorious reward. He bequeathed to De La Salle his Institute of the Daughters of the Holy Child Jesus. Faithfully did he keep the sacred trust confided to him by the dying priest. He procured them *letters patent*, had their public utility recognized and acknowledged by the City Council, and ceased not to labor in their behalf till the Daughters of the Child Jesus were firmly established. Well might he be considered their protector and second founder.

One day as he approached the convent he was met by two travellers careworn and fatigued ; one was of mature years, the other young. In them, without knowing it, De La Salle was greeting the first laborers in a vineyard over which he was soon to preside. Let us glance at what had been previously done for the education of the poor.

"Primary education begins with the Church. Christ was Himself a teacher of the elements of divine truth which He came to make known to men ; His Apostles were the earliest Christian educators. The Church and the school for the people have always been inseparable. As time rolled on, and revolution followed revolution, the Church clung to her divine mission to ' go and teach!' Even when success crowned her efforts, and princes encouraged her labors, she forgot not her calling. Her sons went forth, formed colonies, and exchanged the comforts of an established home for the miasma of the marsh and the terrors of the forest."

"The pagan world had paid but little if any attention to the instruction of the masses. The Church, on the other hand, had devoted herself unreservedly to the task for sixteen centuries ; her councils obliged to this

by the force of their laws ; chapters of different churches
looked upon it as a first duty, their treasures were
poured out unstintingly in this noble cause : wherever
the Church arose there were found men laboring for
the betterment of mankind, through the elevation of
the standard of intelligence among youth.''

" In her Alexandrian Schools the Christian system
absorbed every branch of learning. . . . In Ireland
' Columba was the first to lead the way in whatever
labors the monks engaged.' Thither, as from a nest,
these sacred doves took their flight to every quarter.
They studied the classics, the mechanical arts, law,
history, and physics. They improved the arts of hus-
bandry, . . . supplied the rude people, whom they had
undertaken to civilize, with ploughshares and other
utensils of labor, and taught them the use of the forge,
in the mysteries of which every Irish monk was in-
instructed from his boyhood."

In France, in 789, an edict was published, requiring
elementary schools to be attached to all monasteries
and Catholic churches, *without exception,* and that children of all ranks, both rich and poor, should be received therein. The more important monasteries were
to open High Schools, in which mathematics, astrono-
my, arithmetic, geometry, music and rhetoric would be
taught.

When the Venerable De La Salle undertook to form
his first disciples, primary education was at a low ebb
in his native country. The methods of instruction
were wearisome and hampering. He drew up clear,
simple, and effective plans ; carrying these plans out,
his schools rapidly became successful. At first this
breaking from old established usages roused a fierce
spirit of opposition against him. Calumnies and per-

secutions followed. A heart less devoted to the welfare of youth might have wavered in this trying ordeal, but De La Salle, following meekly in the footsteps of the Saviour, rejoiced to suffer in so holy a cause. It may, indeed, be said that the love of suffering was one of his distinctive characteristics. During the forty years which were spent in laying the lasting foundation of his work, many and grievous were his trials, but never a murmuring word fell from his lips, and never did his confidence in the divine protection weaken.

The Venerable De La Salle gave repeated instances of his humility. He looked upon himself as one destined to labor as the servant of all. If a Brother fell sick, he hastened to replace him in the class room, where he was distinguished by the gentleness of his bearing, the charity of his proceedings, and the zeal which marked his every movement. He considered the office of Christian teacher " a most noble one and most necessary to the Church," and highly meritorious in the sight of God, as may be seen in the decrees of councils, and the example of the saints. This employment, he felt, particularly demanded the fulness of the spirit of faith, since without it, an office so august and divine in its bearings, becomes merely secular to the carnal eye. He desired that the Brothers should look upon themselves as the spiritual fathers of their pupils, the co-operators of Jesus Christ; imitators of the apostles, and of the greatest doctors, who considered it a singular happiness to be employed in the nurseries of the Church and society in which youth is brought up in the fear of the Lord, and the practice of every moral and social virtue. It is only this spirit of faith which can induce the Brother of the Christian Schools to look upon his class as a safe asylum, a re-

fuge in which young souls, threatened with shipwreck
at every moment, may seek a safe harbor from the
storms of uprising passions, and the force of the waves
of evil habits.

He touchingly dwells on the reward the Brothers
will receive for their labor. "Oh, what happiness," he
exclaims, " is in store for a good Brother of the
Christian Schools ! What shall be his feelings when,
surrounded by his numerous pupils, all like himself
safe in their eternal home, they will admit that through
the merits of Jesus Christ, applied through their masters, they have been saved. What unalloyed rejoicing shall then be seen between master and pupils. What
an union, in God, between souls gathered in the bonds
of love and gratitude ! What happiness he shall ex-
perience conversing upon *the riches of his inheritance in
the saints.*

" The crown shall be proportioned to the labor sus-
tained, the victories won, the fatigues endured. Hence
all these trials may be considered as so many sources
of rejoicing. Our zeal must herein find food upon
which to strengthen itself against difficulties, obstacles,
and persecutions. After such a career, the true Brother will be able unceasingly to proclaim in a better
land : ' *I exceedingly abound with joy,* because *of all our
tribulations.*' "

Thus feeling, and thus inspiring his disciples to
feel, what did the Venerable De La Salle accomplish ?
Let us glance at the various classes of teaching
he inaugurated. Here is the summary made by
the Inspector General of Education in France, who
says : '· The illustrious Founder of the Brothers of the
Christian Schools was the pioneer of popular education, not only in France but in all Europe. With one

master-stroke he founded seminaries for country
teachers, normal institutions for city masters, boarding schools in which everything relating to commerce,
finance, military engineering, architecture, and mathematics was taught, ... and in which trades could be
learned. Finally, an institution in which agriculture
was taught as a science. In one word, the Abbé De
La Salle, at a single casting, brought forth from the
mould schools for the poor, primary normal colleges,
superior or higher training schools for specific subjects,
technical institutions, agricultural colleges, in which
last the cultivation of land was studied on a scientific
basis."

The boarding school at St. Yon, near Rouen, was
opened at the urgent request of wealthy parents who
insisted that their children should be allowed to pro-
fit by the excellent teaching of the Brothers of La Salle.
In 1698 Louis XIV. sent the sons of the exiled Irish
officers of the army of James II. to De La Salle as the
best educator in France. In this school the young
gentlemen received an education in accordance with
their rank and which enabled them to fill ably the
various ·offices of trust for which they were destined.

We have seen how far ahead of all elementary schools
were those of De La Salle in his time. The Institute
has not degenerated. Its schools for the people are
still the best, not only in France, but throughout the
civilized world.

Much as this benefactor has done for society, we but
partially understand his character and appreciate his
motives till we lift the veil of modesty and humility
with which he screened his inner life from the gaze of
the world. Much as we admire the work he established, we shall only fully measure its extent and meaning

when we follow the holy Founder into his chamber, watch him at prayer, or shudder at the sight of his self-imposed mortifications. Greatly as we admire the wisdom of his rule, its spirit, its full bearing will only become known when we learn that most of its precepts were determined after long and weary vigils in which the blood of sacrifice was added to the lever of meditation. Greatly as we admire the wisdom of his school regulations and methods, we can only seize upon and grasp their ample bearing and the blessing which attaches to their adoption when we learn that the Venerable was accustomed to remain for hours motionless, entirely absorbed in the study of his disciples in the class-room, after which he retired to his cell, and having implored the light of heaven by fervent prayer, then formed laws for the guidance of his teachers, laws of such consummate wisdom that they have never been equalled.

We have seen the great and useful work of the Venerable accomplished; it now remains to find by what means beyond mere human skill and intelligence he attained such wonderful success.

Before preaching, all the saints exemplified in their own lives the truths and virtues which they exhorted others to embrace. Before giving his spiritual children the Spirit of Faith as the characteristic virtue of their state, he was himself the just man who lives by faith. Faith was the ruling motive which made him see and adore God in all things. This virtue preserved him from the snares into which so many of his day fell through the wiles of Jansenism. It was his loving, lively faith in the Church, and the teachings of her Supreme Pontiff, that made him accept the declarations of the Holy See, even when his own ecclesiastical superiors

delayed in their submission. "ROMAN PRIEST" was
the common title which he added to his name, that
all might know his attachment to the chair of Peter,
and his dying injunction to his children was that
"they should never fail in their devotedness to
Rome." Though a doctor of divinity, he carefully
avoided all unnecessary discussion of disputed points
yet when called upon to make open profession of his
faith, pen and tongue combined to make known his
sentiments. Silent as he usually was under calumny
and reproach, he never suffered his devotion to the
Church to be questioned. Among the few letters he
wrote in self-defence, the most powerful was that in
which he declared his abhorrence of the new doctrine,
his inviolable attachment to the faith and doctrine of
the holy Roman Apostolic Church. Unmoved, he saw
his prosperous novitiate of Marseilles closed by Jansenists, rather than comply in the least with their demands.
The innovators knew well that if they could get so
efficient a body of teachers in their interests their evil
work would be greatly advanced. Thanks, under God,
to the zeal of the holy Founder, and the obedience of
his children, the poison of Jansenism never entered
the institute of the Brothers of the Christian Schools.
Not satisfied with writing and exhorting, the venerable
servant of God offered up not only prayers, but severe
penances and mortifications in behalf of the afflicted
Church, and in these he was generously joined by all
his spiritual children.

But to have faith and to live by faith are quite different things. To live by faith is to judge nothing, to
determine upon no interprise, to do no action save
through thoughts inspired by this lofty virtue, and by
reasons suggested by Christian motives. It is the

spirit of faith which raises the Christian above himself by filling him with the spirit of Christ Jesus ; it is
the thought of this Divine Saviour, his sentiments, his
dispositions which makes the soul, thus animated, live
in a manner worthy of God, by leading a life altogether
divine.

Thus we find that the Venerable De La Salle looked
upon all things by the light of faith ; everything was
judged by supernatural light; in his views, all things
drew their value from the price placed upon them
when weighed in the scales of this sublime virtue.
Through the influence of this faith by which he was
animated, he found himself raised above the false
notions held by the world, ever on his guard against
human motives, or those dictated by worldly wisdom ;
never imposed upon by personal interests ; ever van-
quishing worldly maxims by the study, of gospel precepts, which he accepted as the unique rule of his
life. From this came his wonderful confidence in
God, which induced him, during days of famine, to sell
his goods and distribute the price thereof to the poor,
reserving nothing for himself or disciples, save that
abiding faith in God of which his heroic conduct was
so convincing a proof.

What the rays are in regard to the sun, confidence
in God is with reference to faith. The one is the
measure of the other, as well as the proof of its existence. It is from faith that hope draws its life, its
nourishment and increase. When faith is weak and
lanquishing, confidence in God is enfeebled ; if faith
be lively and animated, confidence in God will be
grand and heroic.

"What saint," asks the Venerable's biographer,
Père Blain, " had more reason to rely solely upon God

THE VENERABLE DE LA SALLE DISTRIBUTING HIS GOODS TO THE POOR.

in his interprises ? Who was more abused, calumniated, and persecuted than the Founder of the Christian Schools, and who, therefore, had greater need of unlimited confidence in the Divine power and goodness to bring him forth successful and victorious from such combined opposition? Parents, friends, benefactors, superiors and inferiors with one accord seemed united in testing the confidence of the great servant of God. It was in the midst of these trials that his unswerving confidence in the power and goodness of God was shown.

We have already seen the Venerable distributing his fortune to the poor ; the more we consider this heroic act and the disastrous times in which he made the sacrifice, the more clearly we will see his abiding confidence in Him who feeds the birds of the air and who tells us that even the hairs of our head are numbered. His confidence in spiritual matters was not less remarkable. This we perceive in the letters he wrote to his Brothers and other religious, or lay persons who corresponded with him, seeking advice in their interior struggles and difficulties. To all he was accustomed to say that their confidence in God should be in proportion to their spiritual misery. To one of his spiritual daughters who was greatly troubled, he wrote these touching and encouraging words :

" Never allow yourself to be foolishly persuaded that you are forsaken by God ; on the contrary, believe that He is more than ever disposed to receive you into His arms. His mercy manifests itself in proportion to the greatness of your wretchedness. The more abandoned you seemingly are, the more abundantly will His mercies be shown in your favor. He knows the extent of your weakness ; that you require His grace to establish and confirm you, when weakness and cowardice would cause you to lose ground." "Truly," adds the author of "Thoughts of the Venerable De La Salle," "those lessons of confidence in God came with fitting force from the mouth and pen of so patient and confiding a man of God."

The work inaugurated by the Venerable and the devotedness which he manifested for the poor who flocked to his classes sufficiently attest his charity. If any further proof were required, we may find it in the alacrity with which he forgave those who had been guilty of the greatest injustice against him.

De La Salle's life was one continual act of union with God. When he left St. Sulpice he was already noted for his love of mental prayer; his after years saw him constantly growing in the earnestness with which he devoted himself to this holy exercise. It was his constant effort to beget a like spirit among his Brothers. For this purpose he wrote a detailed "Method of Mental Prayer," in which he enters into such minute details that it is impossible for any one, faithful to the precepts of this precious work, to fail to become a man of prayer, after the model of the holy Founder. Of his "Method of Meditation," a learned author has said: "Unfortunately, this explanation is too little known; but his own children can never drink too deeply from the spiritual waters which flow from the sacred source."

A man of prayer and meditation necessarily becomes spiritually enlightened and wise, since his views of things, and the value he places upon them, in every case correspond with those of God. We have ample proof of this in the life of the Venerable De La Salle. His wisdom possessed all the characteristics attributed to that beautiful virtue by Saint Paul.

Its first effect is to inspire one with a singular attraction for purity of heart, body and mind. Now all the historians of his life unite in assuring us that one of the great objects of his spiritual efforts was to preserve this triple purity. He had nothing more at heart, and for this purpose added the most severe mortifications to a ceaseless vigilance over his body and its senses, his mind and its faculties.

The second characteristic of wisdom is to love peace ; to observe order in all one's actions, to make God his sole object. The life of De La Salle fully realized this second trait. Peace reposed in his heart, the smile of a peaceful conscience irradiated his beautiful countenance.

The third characteristic is modesty, for which he was not less remarkable. Speaking of the high degree to which the Venerable practised this virtue, his first historian writes: "In the modesty of this servant of God, I find reproduced the traits which St. Athanasius describes as having been seen in the great St. Athony. Such was the modesty that shone upon his countenance that he was distinguished from all who surrounded him. His sanctity of soul and purity of mind were indicated on his features ; he was ever gay. tranquil, unchanged." The same writer further adds that like St. Bernard, "so well regulated was his whole exterior that every movement was expressive of humility, and at the same time a Christian elegance that inspired respect and caused a feeling of joy in all who beheld him."

Finally, what shall we say of his obedience, for here we must stop our enumeration. Of this crowning virtue we may truly say. after the example of our Divine Lord, he was obedient unto death. As years progressed and his end drew near, his love of this virtue increased. It was in the practice of holy obedience he found his greatest happiness. In his contest over self, in his constant struggle after a more perfect life, he was animated by the fixed hope that being an obedient religious would enable him to speak of victory.

We cannot form a better idea of the holiness of life, the extraordinary degree of perfection to which any great servant of God, any Founder of a religious order has attained, than by studying the lives of his first disciples. The earliest historian of the Institute, in writing of them records that " the first disciples of the Venerable De La Salle who were constant observers of his words and acts, understood that they could not be his spiritual children unless they reproduced his image within themselves, by imitating his virtue. Indeed we find in them the thoughts, the sentiments, the supernatural views and virtues which characterize the Venerable De La Salle." They were not only docile disciples to the instructions and directions of a master to whom they were attached, but emulators of his every virtue. They suffered at times the rudest shocks, but with his invisible patience they pursued the work he inaugurated, confident like him, of the Divine protection over an Institute which, closely united to the chair of Peter, shares its destinies, which are frequently to be buffeted by storm, but never to be submerged.

Glorious indeed is the mission of the Christian Brothers. To quote the words of the Venerable Founder: "They are co-workers with Christ in saving souls." Happy those who are called to this holy life, who are blessed with so exalted a vocation. Here is a timely place to address a few words to the young, ardent, and zealous souls who only need the way opened

to them eagerly to walk therein. Do not your hearts
lean toward a state whose work is to sculpture living
angels from out the block of human nature, presented
by every child who enters a Christian School ? Can
you imagine a cause more worthy of your highest am-
bition than to raise up for God and society a Christian
offspring, which "can only be secured by a Christian
education." Remember that "Christian virtues do
not grow spontaneously in the soul. They are the
result of careful and constant culture ; and this must
begin early in childhood." Can you, dear youth, ask
any grander field in which to labor ? What more lasting source of gratitude can you offer the world, society
at large, than that which you would be entitled to
claim by joining a body to whom is confided the " wonderful privilege of training immortal souls to fulfil the
duties assigned them by their heavenly Father, that
they may receive from His hands an eternal crown in
heaven ?" In such a calling, it will be yours to take
the same care of children " that a skilful gardener
would take of delicate flowers which he knows are highly prized by his master." If it becomes the imperative duty of parents " to send their children to Christian Schools," surely it must be the imperative duty of
others to take upon themselves the task of governing
and teaching these pupils. " The question of religious
education is the paramount question of the day, in the
solution of which. our destiny as a Christian people
must depend ;" so declare the highest authorities in
the Catholic Church in our land. Is there anything
which you, youthful reader, can imagine as higher or
more ennobling than to pursue a vocation which tends
to realize the hopes and wishes, the prayers and com-
mands of prelates alike distinguished for their piety,

learning, and zeal? Think for a moment, what it is to
take part in opening and maintaining Christian
Schools, whose mission is pointed out so forcibly by
the same high authority: "The Catholic school is
the good seed in the hearts of children, to bear in after years glorious fruits for our country and our religion. . . ." In these schools children will learn all
that will make them hereafter loyal citizens of their
country, and valiant soldiers of Christ and His holy
Church. By these schools the efforts of infidelity will
be rendered abortive; by them will religion be forti-
fied; by them will your pastors be able to repeat the
touching words of the Divine Master : " Father, those
whom thou gavest me I have kept, and not one of
them is lost."

In so important a question as that of religious vocation, it is of the greatest moment to understand the subject more fully, and earnestly to pray God to give us
strength to follow when He makes known His divine will.
Do not allow human motives, family interests to inter-
fere. Cast worldly hopes and prospects aside. Compare
the perishable present with the eternal future. Bring
to mind the terrible punishments inflicted on those
who do not obey God. Strive to form an exact idea
of the secular state, with all its trials, dangers, and
transitory rewards and gratifications. Then form an
equally exact idea of the religious state. Study and
strive to appreciate the nine fruits of the religious
life attributed to St. Bernard, and in which that great
doctor and saint of the Church shows how man in holy
religion :

1. Lives more pure ; 2. Falls more rarely ; 3. Rises
more promptly ; 4. Is bedewed by the waters of grace
more frequently ; 5. Passes his life more holily ; 6.

Reposes more securely ; 7. Dies more confidently ; 8. Is released more promptly ; 9. Is rewarded more abundantly.

Such considerations will make you feel the beauty, the loveliness, the worth of a religious state. Bear in mind, youthful reader, it is not a question of greater or lesser good, it is one of salvation. Without following your vocation, there is a *possibility*, but only a possibility of salvation.

The world hungers for the bread of life ; children in multitudes ask for teachers who will feed them with the saving doctrines of Mother Church. Who, called by the Divine voice, can refuse ? Who, with heart beating responsively to the higher and nobler aspirations of Christian heroism, will say " No !" when called upon by the Almighty in words which conscience hears and heart feels, to labor in that grand field, the noblest, the highest, the most acceptable to Mother Church, and therefore to God, the work of Christian education, the great question of the hour."

Stay, youthful reader, before going further in your reading ; offer up a fervent prayer to know whether such is not *your* calling ; and if this be the case, thank the good God ; praise Mary Immaculate through whom this grace has been given you ; and, when, in the happy moment of the accomplishment of your vocation, you are vested in the habit of the Brother of the Christian Schools, say, " 'To God, from whom all blessings flow, be praise !' Thanked be Mary, who has led me to the foot of the altar of sacrifice, where I can best secure the interests of Jesus, the Saviour of men ; grateful offerings be made to my dear angel guardian, who ' from unrighteous ways hath saved me, lest in error's path I stray.' "

Yes, dear youth, such a vocation is one which will give heaven cause to rejoice, not that one sinner has been converted, but that there has been joined to the army of Christian teachers another worker, who will not only teach and direct the ninety-nine who need not penance, but also save the hundredth who has fallen away.

Does not such a mission inspire you? Can you think of the good to be done and yet remain callous? No; such is not the character of the truly Catholic Christian boy. His is a noble disposition, a willing heart, a generous soul—such is yours, youthful reader, if, called by the good God, you put your hand generously to the plough and never turn back, thus proving yourself, "worthy of the kingdom of heaven."

What more glorius task? for two hundred and more years thousands of Brothers of the Christian Schools have devoted themselves to the cause of Christian education. In all that time heaven has been peopled by the souls saved through Christian, religious teaching. Now is the day, now the hour, when more gleaners are called into the vineyard, where "the harvest is great the laborers few." Will you listen to the voice of grace, the call of God? If so, blessed indeed is your lot, for "of such is the kingdom of heaven."

You may hear it said, "It is as well to remain in the world as to enter religion." To this St. Liguori answers : "People of the world make no scruple of telling young persons called to the religious life that they can serve God in every state, even in the midst of the world. Yes, it is quite true that we can serve God in every place, when we are not called to the religious state ; but not when we are called, and we wish to please our own fancy by remaining in the world. In this latter case it is difficult to live well and to serve God." (See " Choice of a State of Life.')

" WHO SHOULD ENCOURAGE, DEVELOP, AND FOSTER RE-LIGIOUS VOCATIONS?"

Every *family*, but, especially every *mother*, every *father*, every *priest*, every *teacher*, and finally every *Christian*, zealous for God's glory and the salvation of souls.

Every Catholic mother should be delighted to offer at least one of her sons as an apostle in a work so dear to the Sacred Heart of Jesus, so prized by holy Mother Church, and so essential to the welfare of society. A son thus consecrated to what is noblest on earth— the Christian education of youth, will be the brightest gem in her crown of glory. Well may she rejoice in the exceeding favor that has been shown her in being the mother of a son so signally blessed. And the Christian father! Should it not be to him the richest reward for his toils and cares that his son is called to so holy a life? Nothing grieves the heart of a good father more than to see his son going astray, and nothing then should delight him more than to see him devoting his whole life to the service of God and his neighbor in the religious state. Such a father may consider himself thrice blessed.

And the Reverend Clergy, first in every good cause, shall they not give a helping hand, speak an encourageing word, where the germs of a vocation appear, or that indications lead to suspect its existence? Who better than the priest knows the value of the religious school ; the importance of having teachers whose whole lives are exclusively devoted to so noble a cause? But we will not urge the question with those devoted ministers of Christ. The words of their own Most Reverend and Right Reverend prelates will be the fittest form of appeal. His Eminence, the Most Rev. Cardinal Archbishop of New York, who has always been most interested in the work of the Brothers, says :

" As it may often be in the power of pastors or confessors to foster and encourage vocations to a life so eminently useful and meritorious as is that of the Christian Brothers, or to recommend fitting subjects for their Novitiate, I am induced to solicit the aid of their influence in this direction, that thus the religious training and education of Catholic children may be more effectually promoted and secured." To this, the Most Reverend Coadjutor's lines, written when directing the See of Newark, may fittingly be added :

" I beg to recommend to you the fostering of vocations for this admirable Institution from which so many benefits accrue to youth, and from which, if vocations be multiplied, we may hope so much more in future for the welfare of religion."

In language inspired by his zeal for the little ones of his fold, the Most Rev. Archbishop of Baltimore also says :

" You are thoroughly convinced of the necessity of a Christian education. It is the only guardian and preservative of the faith of the rising generation. For this reason, the vocations of religious teachers are to be encouraged. Their increase depends, in a great measure, upon you, whose office it is to study the dispositions of youth, and who have the faculty to distinguish those whom Providence seems to call to the noble life of the Christian teacher."

" I bless this work (the new Novitiate of Baltimore) with all my heart,and hope that the reverend clergy will

exercise their solicitude in encouraging vocations to the Institute of the Brothers of the Christian Schools."
—JAMES GIBBONS, *Abp. Baltimore.*

These extracts might suffice, but let us listen to voices hushed in death and whose works speak after them Thus wrote the illustrious Archbishop Spalding: "I beg to enlist your zeal in behalf of the Christian Brothers. who are doing so much towards advancing the cause of Catholic education in this country. As the sphere of their action extends, they necessarily need a large increase in their numbers. Hence I invite you to take an interest in finding suitable candidates for their Novitiate in New York."

The Most Rev. Archbishop Wood, during whose administration so many schools and communities of Christian Brothers were opened, wrote: "You will thus, by securing vocations, greatly advance the interests of religion and education," since, says the Cardinal Archbishop of Melines (Belgium), "the Brothers have never been so much needed as at present."

The late tireless champion of the Church and her rights, Mgr. de Ségur, could not be silent on such a subject: "Let us," he exclaims,"again say what we have so often urged; never has the harvest been greater ; never have the Brothers been called upon to open so many establishments ; never has it been within the power of the priest to encourage the work of securing vocations to greater advantage.

"Let it not be said that the number of vocations is becoming smaller. In the midst of the many souls of your parish, prayer and a conscientious search will discover more than one on whom the Almighty has merciful designs, more than one who is called to join in carrying out the work which is most essential in the

Church. To the priesthood is society indebted for civilization; through those zealous priests who will secure subjects to direct and teach Christian schools shall civilization be preserved. Without such assistance the world would again become barbarian."

In conclusion, let us often unite with all fervor in asking God to raise the veil, to make known the worth and wealth of that field in which "the harvest is great the laborers few."

Were any proof needed of the universal interest felt in the life and work of the Venerable De La Salle, the Feast of the Second Centenary would be ample demonstration. The Brothers intended it to be very quiet, among themselves only, but the Christian world at large would not consent to such an arrangement. Parents, pastors, prelates, nay, even the Holy Father thought rightly, that the Second Centenary of a work whose external results are shown by 13,000 religious, guiding 400,000 pupils, was worthy of public recognition. Hence we find the able Superior General, Brother Irlide, saying:

"The celebration of the Second Centenary assumed proportions, and was attended with a degree of pomp and earnestness which we could not possibly foresee, and which we certainly never desired." Elsewhere he continues : "It could not be otherwise, since, from the beginning, both secular and regular clergy were among the special patrons of the Venerable De La Salle. He belonged to the secular clergy of Rheims, many of whom gave essential help to the struggling Institute. The ancient abbey of the Benedictines welcomed him to pray near the tomb of St. Remigius, where he planned his work. The Carmelites also offered the servant of God an asylum among them in

1684, to make a retreat before pronouncing vows of obedience and stability with twelve of his disciples."

And had the limits of a short circular letter permitted, the worthy Superior might have added that the children of St. Dominic offered him bread, while the sons of St. Ignatius defended his reputation against the Jansenists, and enabled him to perpetuate his work in Marseilles.

It was in 1875 that grateful France did honor to herself by erecting at Rouen a statue to his memory. "Deputations from all parts of France, many officers of State, generals of the army, priests without number, bishops with the Cardinal Prelate of Rouen at their head—all vied with one another in doing honor to the good and pious priest, De La Salle, whose whole life was devoted to Christian education. This gorgeous throng of the great of the earth was increased by numerous deputations of modest black-robed men, who had given up all in order to carry out the instructions of their Founder, and to obey the advice of Christ to the rich young man, the better to serve Him and His poor. These men were Christian Brothers. France is justly proud of these humble Christian teaches, and indeed the whole world owes them so much that it shares in her pride and heartily applauds the generouspeople of Rouen who so nobly commemorated their illustrious citizens."

The following from the panegyric delivered by the eloquent Bishop Benson will be interesting :

" It is in the name of the poor, the lowly, the children of the people," of the dearest portion of the church. " that I here apply to the Venerable De La Salle the prophecy of Daniel ; it is in their name that I salute the rising star which will soon be above us in a galaxy of the Church. He is entitled to the double diadem awarded by the great Apostle, as well as by the prophet, to those who labor in word and doctrine (I. Tim. v. 17). To-day it is Rouen that raises a statue and crowns it. The day is not distant when Rome will place on his brow the nimbus of the blessed. . . . The life of the Venerable is a model, his rule a law, his work the glory of France, and of the entire Church. We may therefore take time by the forelock, and, speaking the language of the younger generations, dilate upon the saint who for two centuries has labored in two worlds for the amelioration and salvation of humanity."

Speaking of the results of the Second Centenary celebration, an eminent writer says :

"Considered from the standpoint that God does all things well, the celebration of the Second Centenary of the work of the Venerable De La Salle, bears upon its face evident marks of a Providential influence. When we behold the untold splendor with which the memory of the Christian Brothers' Founder has been celebrated, we cannot fail herein to find a public expression of the wish, thus so fittingly made known, that the cause of the Canonization of John Baptist De La Salle should be pursued with all possible alacrity."

How great this desire may be inferred from the fact thus referred to by Rev. Brother Irlide, who says :

"More than one hundred and fifty Cardinals, Patriarchs, Archbishops, and Bishops, from every quarter of the globe, have sent us letters, which we are to forward collectively to the Holy Father, in which they ask that renewed efforts shall be made to hasten the final honors to our Venerable Founder."

Doubtless inspired by the sentiments of Albany's first Bishop, the present worthy incumbent wrote:

MONUMENT ERECTED AT ROUEN TO THE VENERABLE DE LA SALLE.

"Most Holy Father, a Prince of your Court, an Archbishop, seven Bishops, and two hundred and fifty priests have joined the Brothers and their pupils in celebrating the Second Centenary of De La Salle's work. The only drawback to the festal day, one that was universally felt, was, that in publicly praising the work, we could not publicly invoke the worker. . . . . "

That these requests have been favorably heard appears from the subjoined document:

ROUEN.

DECREE, FOR THE BEATIFICATION AND CANONIZATION OF THE VENERABLE SERVANT OF GOD, JOHN BAPTIST DE LA SALLE, FOUNDER OF THE CONGREGATION OF THE BROTHERS OF THE CHRISTIAN SCHOOLS.

By decree of the Sacred Congregation of Rites, dated May 23, 1879, Our Most Holy Father, Pope Leo XIII., graciously conceded that the validity of the processes ordered by Apostolic authority regarding three miracles, said to have been wrought by God, through the intercession of the aforesaid venerable servant of God, John Baptist De La Salle, be examined in an ordinary meeting of said Sacred Congregation without the intervention and *votum* of the consultors.

Accordingly, the Most Eminent and Most Reverend Cardinal, John Baptist Pitra, the *ponens* in the aforesaid cause, at the instance of Rev. Brother Robustin, Procurator-General of the Congregation of the Brothers of the Christian Schools and postulator of this cause, at a special ordinary meeting of the Sacred Congregation of Rites, appointed according to particular instructions of Our Most Holy Father, published November

20, 1878, and convened at the Vatican on the day here-below stated, proposed the following *dubium*, viz., whether the validity of the processes instituted by Apostolic authority with regard to the miracles in the dioceses of Rouen, Paris and Orleans is well established; whether the witnesses were duly and rightly examined ; and whether the laws alleged were legitimately applied in the case in point, and with the effect for which they were intended. Thereupon the same said Congregation having carefully weighed the matter in all its parts, and having heard the opinion and read the *votum* of the Rev. Augustin Caprara, Promoter of the Faith, gave answer in the affirmative. *Affirmative seu constare.*

DE LA SALLE'S POWER IN HEAVEN.

Great is the power of God as manifested in his saints. In few cases has this power been more forcibly seen than in the cures effected through the Venerable servant of God, John Baptist De La Salle. We select the following from a mass of evidence and a large number of equally authenticated miraculous occurrences.

In the city of Orleans, France, in the year 1832, Miss Victoire Ferry was acting as nurse in the general hospital for the insane. One day while walking in the halls of the institution, she was suddenly attacked by a violent patient and kicked with such severity that she must have been killed had not two other patients come to her assistance. She was carried to her room unconscious and shortly after, blood flowed copiously from her mouth, ears and nostrils. She trembled convulsively, and all indications pointed to a complete internal disorganization. Ordinary remedies proving of no avail, Dr. Vallet was called in and declared that serious injury had been received in the region of the heart. He prescribed bleeding, leechings and various medicines. For two years, this course was pursued, without avail ; she was unable to work, lost her sleep and became greatly emaciated. To meet the new developments in her case, blisters and other approved remedies were prescribed, yet no relief came. To intensify her case, vomitings of blood became frequent. Finally she was unable to walk or even to stand, and had to remain either in bed or seated in a reclining chair. Thus, for twelve years did she suffer, while, for the last eight, the symptoms had been alarming. Fever seldom left her ; she swallowed food with great difficulty, and drink of the simplest kinds produced vomiting. During this prolonged illness she was bled two hundred and twelve times, and over one hundred useless attempts had been made to bleed her. Her first medical attendant (Dr. Vallet) had long since given up her case, but, in 1839, another physician attended her for two or three months without giving any hopes of relief, as the principal organs, and especially the heart, having been effected for several years, a remedy was physically impossible. She frequently swooned away in her mother's arms, and so great was the swelling in her body that when touched, the mark of the fingers remained on the flesh.

Man had done all in his power, and Miss Ferry now had recourse to our Blessed Lady and her favorite saints. But God's designs were to be realized : it was left to the Venerable De La Salle to manifest his power in her extraordinary case.

Having learned that this great servant of God had obtained many extraordinary cures for his devout clients, Miss Ferry began to invoke him on the 18th of May, 1844. The Brothers of the Christian Schools of Orleans united with her in the novena she began on that day. Holding in her hand a picture and a relic of the Venerable she said :

" Good Father : Venerable servant of God, John Baptist De La Salle, pray for me who have recourse to thee. If it be God's holy will, obtain my cure. If, on the contrary, I am to die, willingly do I resign myself, that my soul may be sanctified." This prayer she repeated, day and night, either mentally, or vocally as her strength permitted. Sunday, the 19th of May, she felt the most excruciating pains over her whole body, and towards half past seven in the evening, though she saw no one, yet she heard a voice distinctly saying : "*Next Sunday, at a quarter to eight, you will hear holy Mass in thanksgiving for your recovery. Keep silent on this subject.*" She had previously tried to read an abridgement of the Venerable's life and now perused it to the end. This effort increased her sufferings, which became so intense that she could not bear even to be touched, while being waited upon. Such was her restlessness that she was placed seated in an arm chair, where she remained most of the time ; and thus she continued in intense agony the first two days of the novena.

On the 20th, she imagined that some one was touching her feet and knees, but a diligent search revealed nothing. Strange to relate, though the picture of the Venerable servant of God had been dropped during the search, she found it again between her hands without knowing how it came there. Thus matters rested till the hour of midnight tolled. At that moment she beheld at her right the Venerable, who said to her :

"*I am John Baptist De La Salle.*" " *Oh, Venerable Father,*" she replied, "*I am not worthy that you should appear to me.*" " *On Sunday,*" he continued, " *at a quarter to eight, you will go to Mass in thanksgiving for your recovery. Be silent on this subject : you are now cured.*" " *Good Father,*" responded the grateful woman, " *I thank you for all the favors you have bestowed upon me. I know and acknowledge that I am unworthy of them.*" At the same moment, she who had for twelve years been a victim to every pain, whose case had long since been abandoned as incurable by the ablest physicians, felt herself completely at rest, free from any pain, and passed the balance of the night in a peaceful slumber. The next morning, she dressed herself, fell upon her knees to thank God, and immediately after her devotions, attended to some manual labor. . . . . Thus she continued till the following Sunday, when, unaided, she walked to Church, to receive holy Communion. As she entered the sacred edifice, though she had no thought of the matter to time her movements, the tower clock struck a quarter to eight. Six physicians testified to the miraculous character of the cure, and Miss Ferry was called repeatedly before the ecclesiastical examiners appointed to take evidence. Their opinion agreed with that of the physicians, and her case has been sent to Rome for final decision by the highest tribunals.

.

www.ingramcontent.com/pod-product-compliance
Lightning Source LLC
Chambersburg PA
CBHW021549270326
41930CB00008B/1436